T0199136

Two Peas in a Pod

Alisha Mutch

Illustrated by Brian Rivera

WestBow Press books may be ordered through booksellers or by contacting:

WestBow Press
A Division of Thomas Nelson & Zondervan
1663 Liberty Drive
Bloomington, IN 47403
www.westbowpress.com
844-714-3454

Because of the dynamic nature of the Internet, any web addresses or links contained in this book may have changed since publication and may no longer be valid. The views expressed in this work are solely those of the author and do not necessarily reflect the views of the publisher, and the publisher hereby disclaims any responsibility for them.

ISBN: 978-1-6642-7443-3 (sc)
ISBN: 978-1-6642-7445-7 (hc)
ISBN: 978-1-6642-7444-0 (e)

Library of Congress Control Number: 2022914120

Print information available on the last page.

WestBow Press rev. date: 08/05/2022

WESTBOW
PRESS®
A DIVISION OF THOMAS NELSON
& ZONDERVAN

This book is dedicated to my sweet boys, Caleb and Connor, who gave me the incredible experience of being a twin mama and having two to hold and love. May God bless both of you always.

Two twins, two twins
As different as can be.
Born of the same womb
With unique personalities.

One is tall and slender,
The other shorter and more stout,
But, both have blue eyes and blonde hair
Which brings a smile to their mother's mouth.

Two tow-headed precious little boys,
Made in God's very image,
Two peas in a pod just
Couldn't be more different.

This one likes to run fast,
The other takes his time.
Both end up in the same place,
By his own style and design.

Two twins, two twins
As different as can be.
Born of the same womb
With unique personalities.

This one is calm and mellow
While the other has more pizzazz.
But, both express their feelings
In a style no one can match.

This one likes all the colors
While the other prefers blue.
And both agree they love pink
When sissy is in the room.

That one loves his two piglets
While the other loves glitz and glam,
So, it's fun to imagine just what
Will happen as they move ahead.

Two twins, two twins
As different as can be.
Born of the same womb
With unique personalities.

Twins are individuals
no matter the time or day.
They love to go opposite directions
Yet momma prays they both will follow God's way.

By God's design though born the same day,
Both are set apart, each in their own way.
Precious twins you be,
A special bond you share.

You are both one-of-a-kind,
Amazing and talented masterpieces
Sent down from Heaven above
To grace this earth
And leave your own mark,
Both as a twin
And as an individual set apart.

Two tow-headed precious little boys
Made in God's very image.
Two peas in a pod just
Couldn't be more different.

Two twins, two twins
As different as can be.
Born of the same womb
With unique personalities.

Although you are two peas in a pod
Who couldn't be more different,
God gave you a special bond
As twin brothers forever.
That was His intent.

Printed in the United States
by Baker & Taylor Publisher Services